HARMONICA *Listen & Learn*
HOMESPUN MUSIC INSTRUCTION

John
SEBASTIAN
TEACHES
Blues Harmonica

A Complete Guide
for Beginners

Cover photos by Dion Ogust

Audio Editor: George James

Mastered by: Ted Orr at
Nevessa Productions, Woodstock, N.Y.

ISBN 0-7935-6047-0

EXCLUSIVELY DISTRIBUTED BY

HAL•LEONARD
CORPORATION
7777 W. BLUEMOUND RD. P.O. BOX 13819 MILWAUKEE, WI 53213

CD instruction makes it easy! Find the section of the lesson you want with the press of a finger; play that segment over and over until you've mastered it; easily skip over parts you've already mastered—no clumsy rewinding or fast-forwarding to find your spot; listen with the best possible audio fidelity; follow along track-by-track with the book.

John SEBASTIAN TEACHES Blues Harmonica
A Complete Guide for Beginners

A Note From John Sebastian

Dear Homespun student,

This CD comes to you with thanks to the people whose requests created it. Ever since The Lovin' Spoonful, half of the after-concert crowd has come with questions about the harmonica. The little instrument, perhaps originally intended to play Tyrolean folk tunes, has gotten a whole new audience as a result of its evolution as one of the main tools of the blues.

The great masters—from Will Shade to Jazz Gillum, from Sonny Boy to DeFord Bailey— have pushed the limits of the harmonica with some startling results. With the help of Happy Traum, guitarist extraordinaire, teacher and all-around jugbandy guy, I've tried to explain some of these techniques.

I hope this CD and book will provide you with some answers....or at least a few new questions.

John Sebastian

Notes On The C Harmonica

Exhaled (Blown) Notes

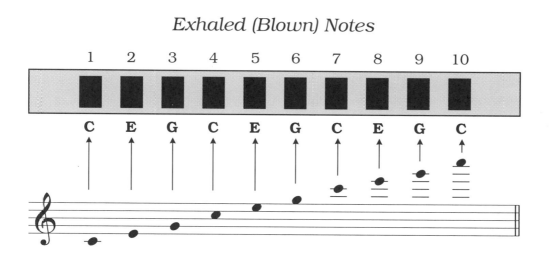

Inhaled (Drawn) Notes

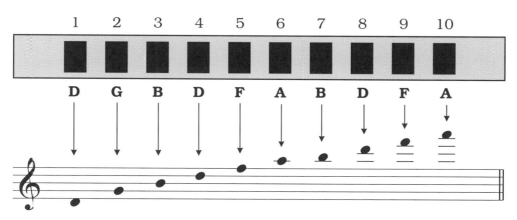

❷ Holding the Harmonica

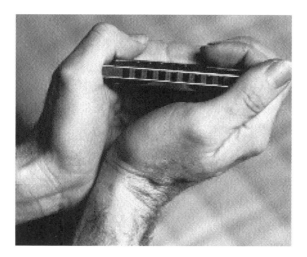

◆3 Whistle Blow Technique

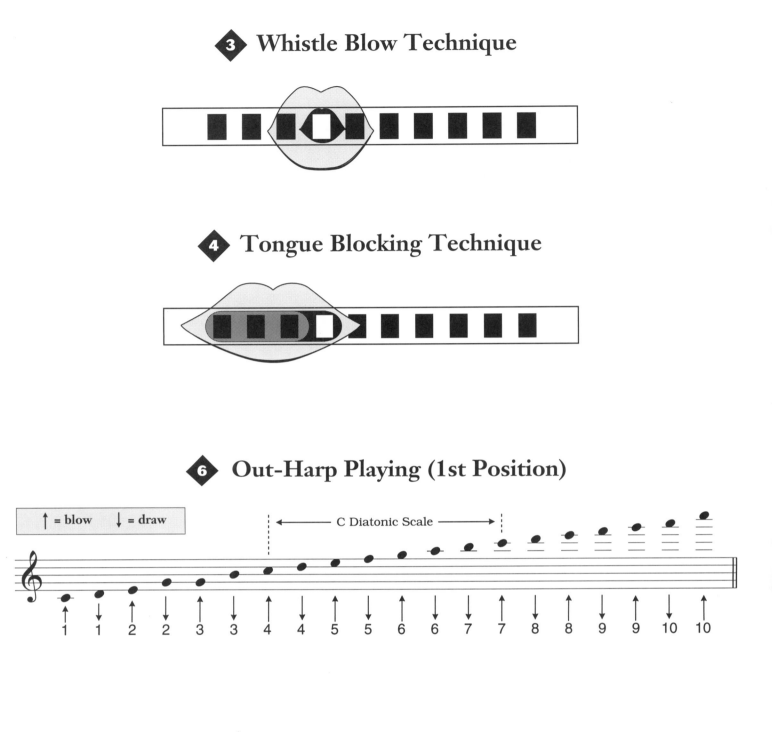

◆4 Tongue Blocking Technique

◆6 Out-Harp Playing (1st Position)

↑ = blow   ↓ = draw

C Diatonic Scale

◆7 "Cowboy" Harmonica

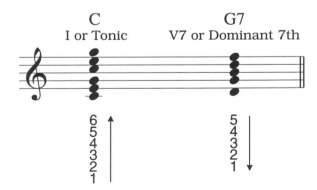

C
I or Tonic

G7
V7 or Dominant 7th

◆8 Streets Of Laredo

Moderately Slow

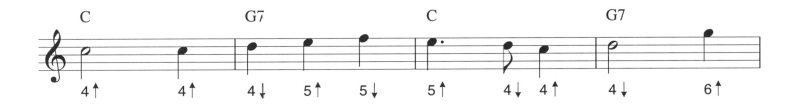

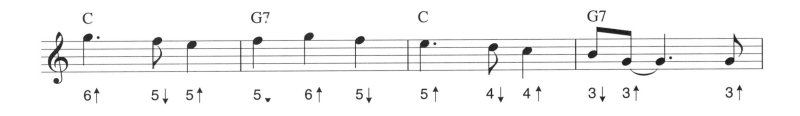

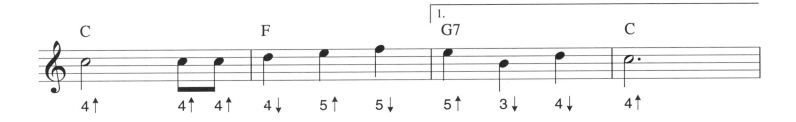

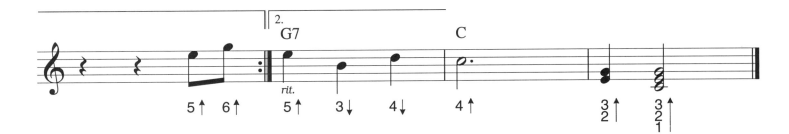

◆9 Basic Chord Theory – I, IV, V7

The primary chords in each key are based on the first, fourth and fifth notes of the diatonic scale. Technically, these are called the *tonic, sub-dominant,* and *dominant* (or *dominant seventh)* chords, but most people refer to them by numbers (often written in Roman numerals): I, IV, and V or V7. The seventh note of the scale (flatted 1/2 step) is usually added to the dominant chord because its sound leads your ear back to the tonic. The tonic – also called the *root* chord, has the same letter name as the key you're in.

Key	Tonic (I)	Sub-Dominant (IV)	Dominant 7th (V7)
C	C	F	G7
D	D	G	A7
E	E	A	B7
F	F	B♭	C7
G	G	C	D7
A	A	D	E7
B♭	B♭	E♭	F7
B	B	E	F♯7

Out-Harp (1st Position)
Using a C Harmonica

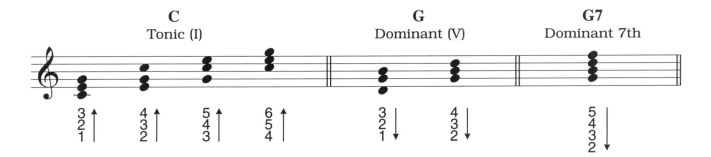

Cross-Harp (Tonic Inhaled)

Normally, the key the harmonica is named for refers to the scales or chords that you get when you blow into it. Blowing into a "C" harp produces a C scale or chord. However, blues players use the *inhaled* chord (normally the dominant) as the tonic. This chart will tell you which harps you will need to play in any given blues key.

Key	Tonic (I)	Sub-Dominant (IV)	Dominant 7th (V7)
C	G	C	D7
D	A	D	E7
E	B	E	F♯7
F	C	F	G7
G	D	G	A7
A	E	A	B7
B♭	F	B♭	C7
B	F♯	B	C♯7

Cross-Harp (2nd Position)
Using a C Harmonica

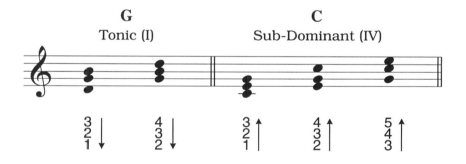

This example starts by drawing the air through hole 4 on the harmonica. To bend this D note down to C♯, raise the middle of your tongue near the roof of your mouth. This will restrict the air flow, thus lowering the pitch of the note. Next, return your tongue to its relaxed position and the pitch will return to D.

Figure 1

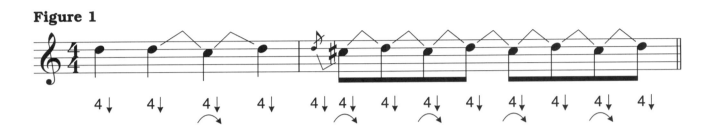

This example consists of a series of *pre-bent* notes. To begin, make sure that the middle of your tongue is near the roof of your mouth before you start to inhale. This causes the first note to be choked. The next note is played with your tongue in its relaxed position. The small notehead in parenthesis is the pitch that the note was before bending. Pre-bends are shown as an upward curving arrow in tablature.

Figure 2

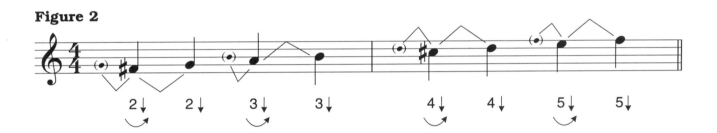

Bending Notes – Exhaled

Using a G Harmonica à la Jimmy Reed

This example starts by blowing the air through hole 8 on the harmonica. To bend this B note down to A♯, use your tongue in the same manner you did when you bent the notes while inhaling.

Figure 1

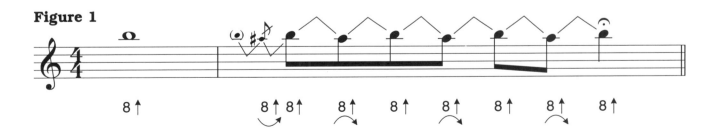

Figure 2

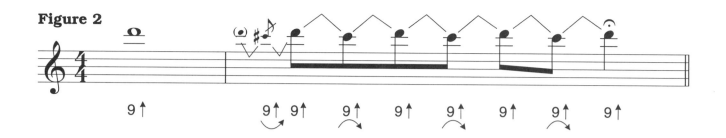

Figure 3

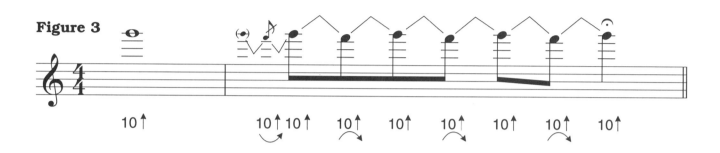

Blues Lick

Using a G Harmonica (1st Position)

⑫ Jimmy Reed-esque Simple Blues

Playing in G on a C Harmonica (2nd Position)

Moderate Shuffle (♫ = ♩♪)

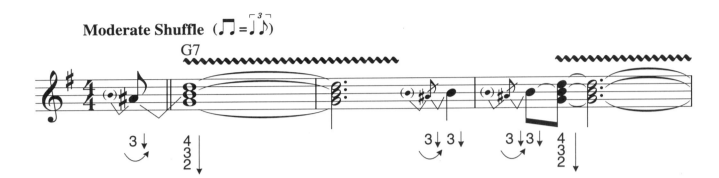

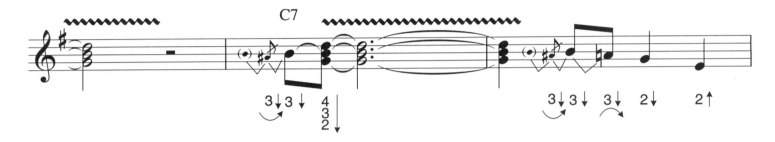

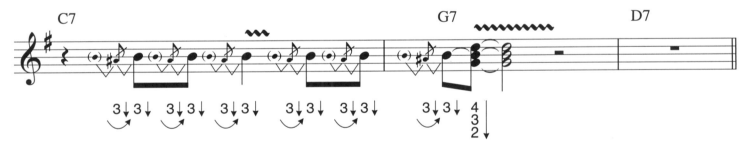

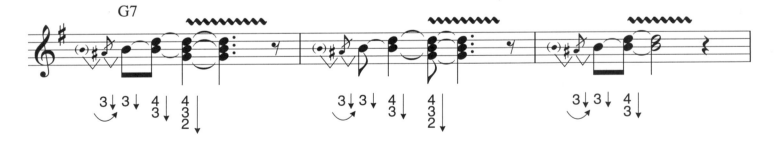

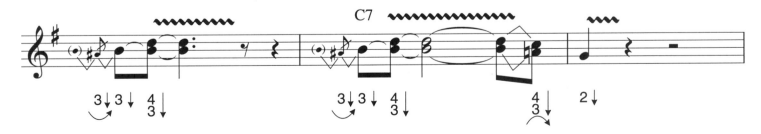

12

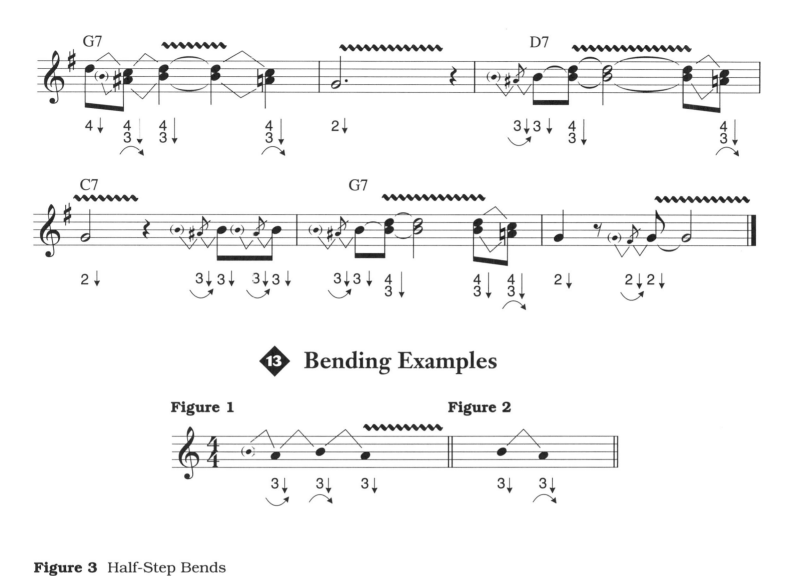

◆13 Bending Examples

Figure 1 **Figure 2**

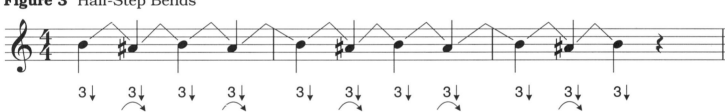

Figure 3 Half-Step Bends

Figure 4 Whole-Step Bends

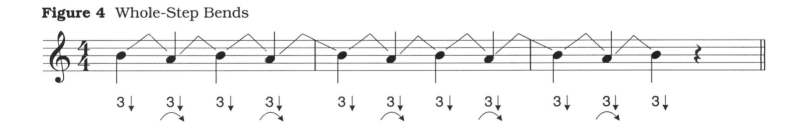

◆14 Basic Lick

Bend and Slide Down

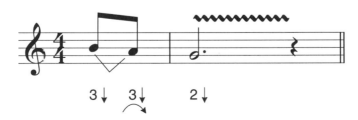

◆14 Simple Blues In G

Bend and Slide Down

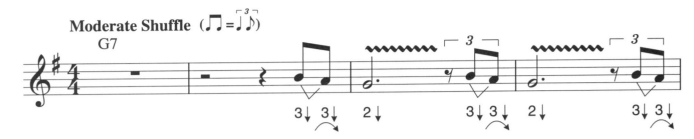

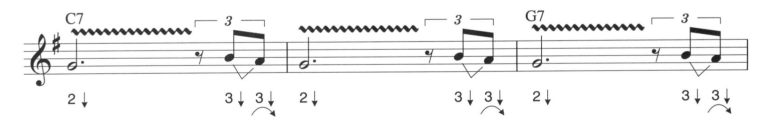

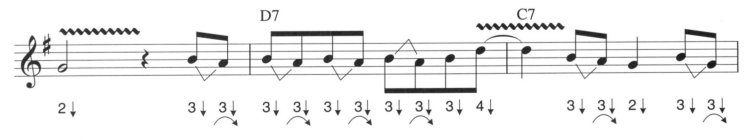

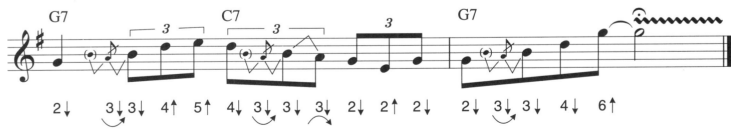

Basic Lick

Pre-Bend and Slide Up

◆ 15 Simple Blues In G

Bend and Slide Up

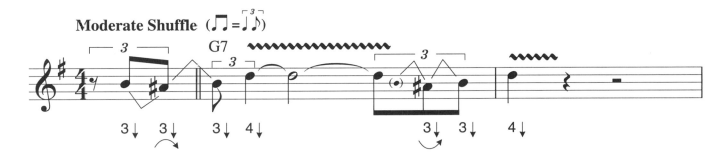

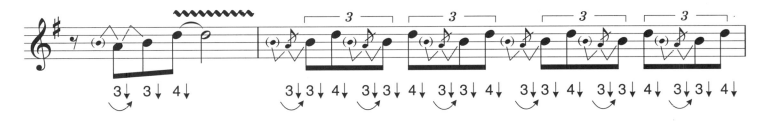

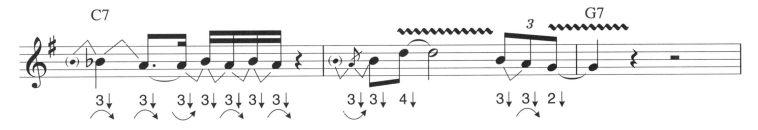

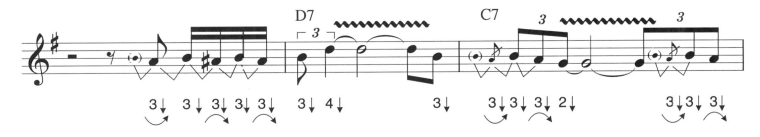

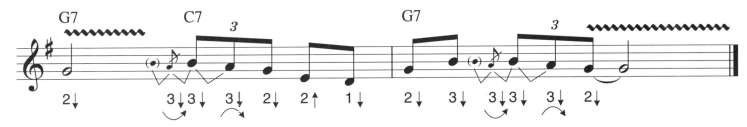

◆16 12-Bar Blues

Using Holes 2, 3 and 4

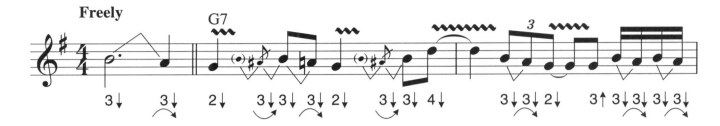

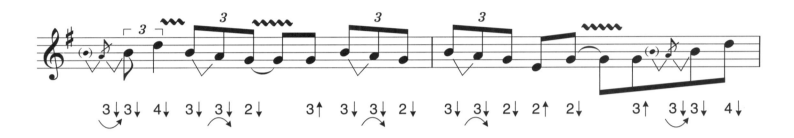

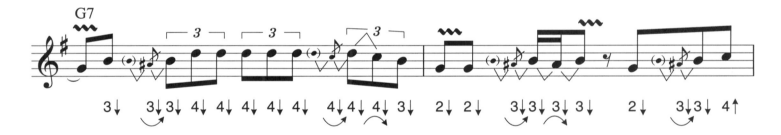

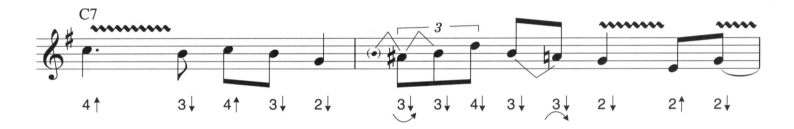

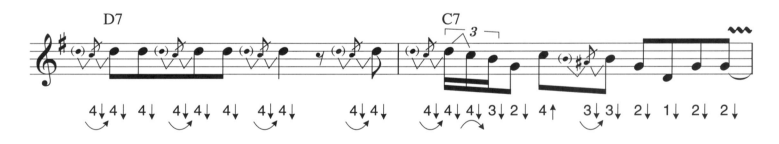

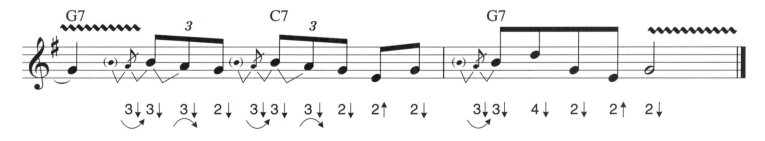

⟨17⟩ Double Note Bending

Figure 1 Holes 1 and 2   **Figure 2** Holes 2 and 3

Figure 3 Holes 3 and 4   **Figure 4** Holes 3 and 5

Country Fiddle Lick

⟨18⟩ Vibrato Technique

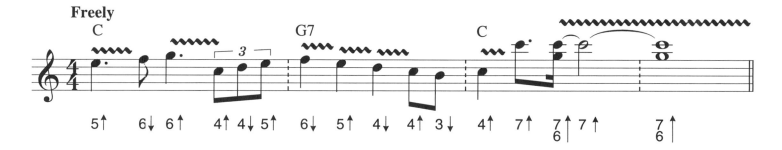

◆20 Oh! Susanna

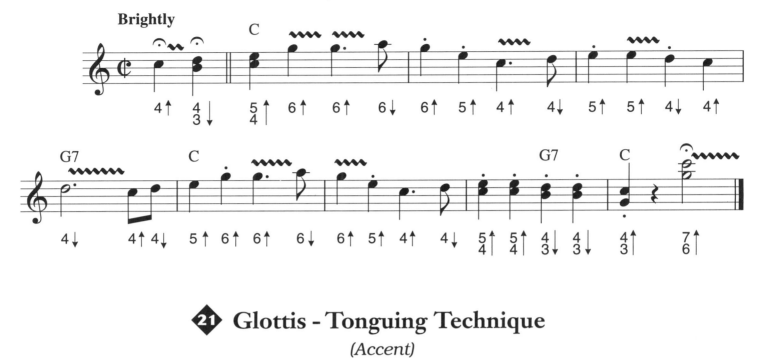

◆21 Glottis - Tonguing Technique

(Accent)

Blues Lick In G

Using the Glottis - Tonguing Technique

Glottis Growl Technique

(Tremolo)

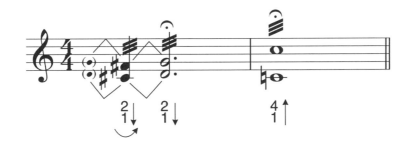

Blues Lick In G

Using Glottis - Tonguing and Growl

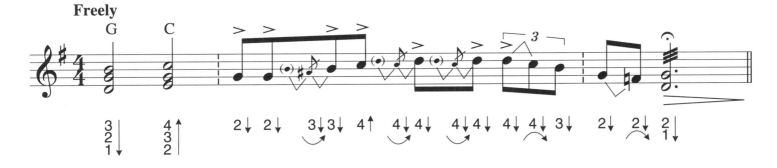

22 Playing In Minor Keys

Minor: 3rd Degree of Chord Dropped 1/2 Step

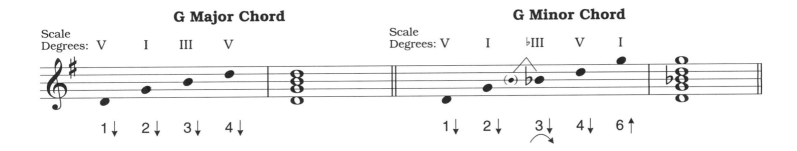

Playing In E Minor

Using a C Harmonica

E Minor Chord

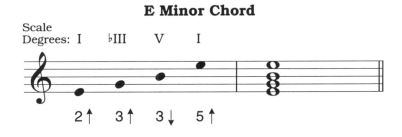

Scale
Degrees: I   ♭III   V   I

2↑   3↑   3↓   5↑

23 Plaintive Melody In E Minor

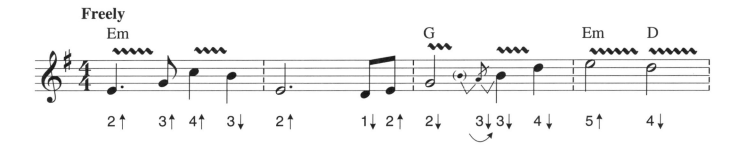

24 Finding the Relative Minor

Using the '50s Chord Progression

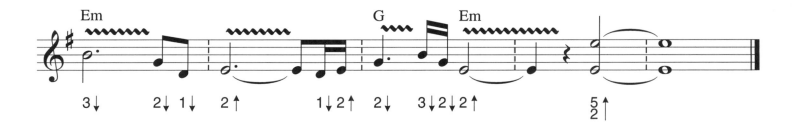

Key	I	vi	IV	V7
C	C	Am	F	G7
G	G	Em	C	D7
		Relative Minor		

25 '50s Style E Minor Melody

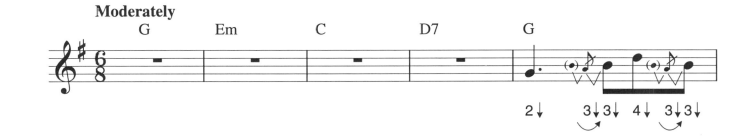

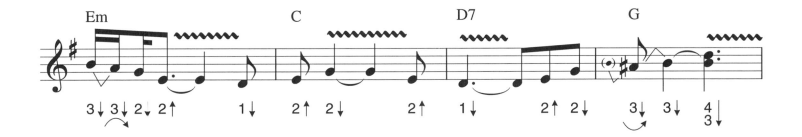

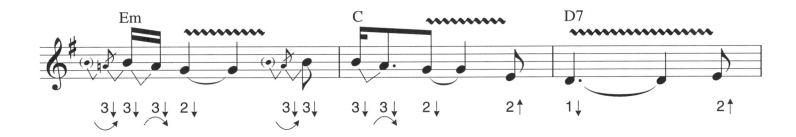

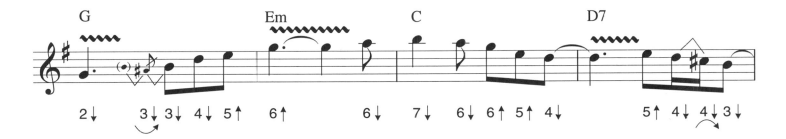

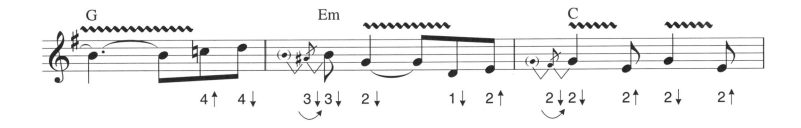

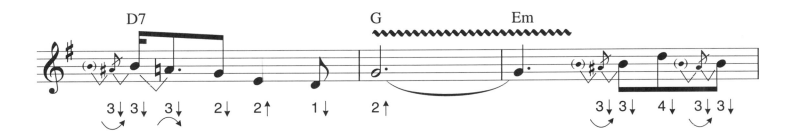

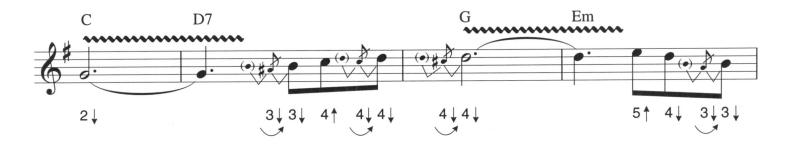

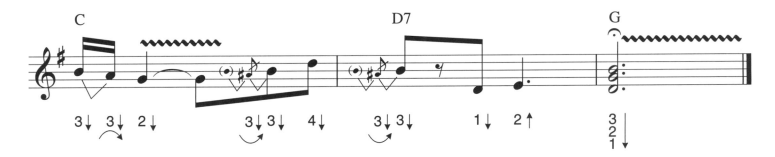

◆26 Technique Solo

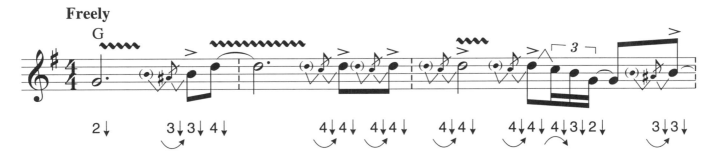

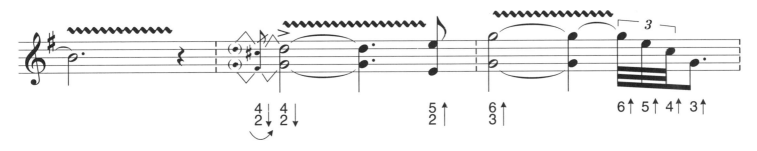

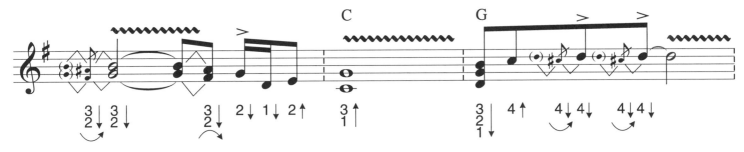

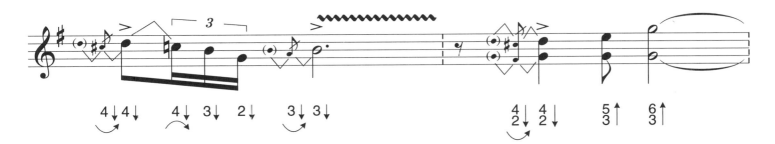

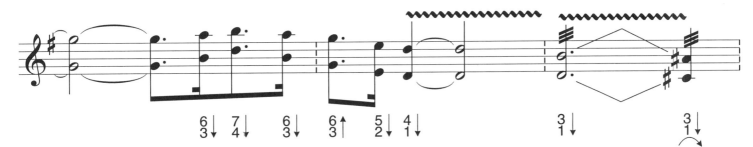

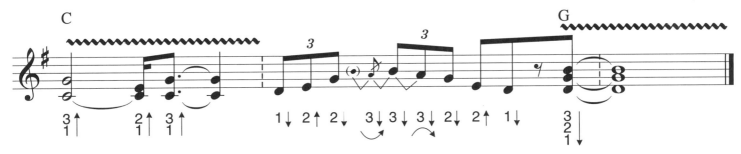

28 Fox Chase Rhythm

◆29 Fox Chase Techniques

Figure 1 Note, Chord, Note, Chord

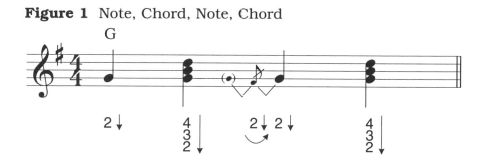

Figure 2 Note, Chord, Chord, Chord

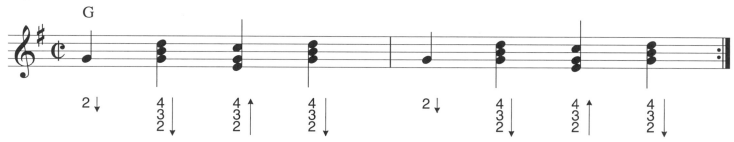

Figure 3 Shuffle

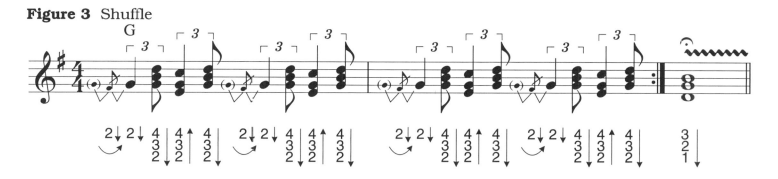

Figure 4 Waltz Time ◆30

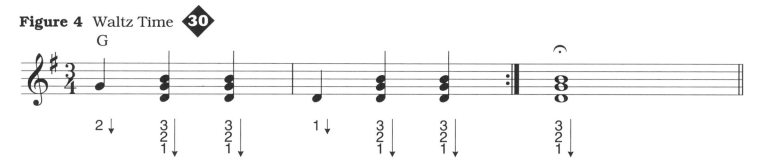

Figure 5 Chord to Single Note ◆31

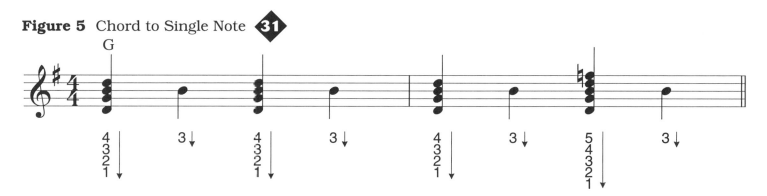

Chord And Note Technique Solo

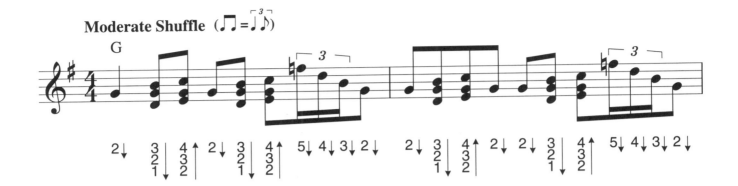

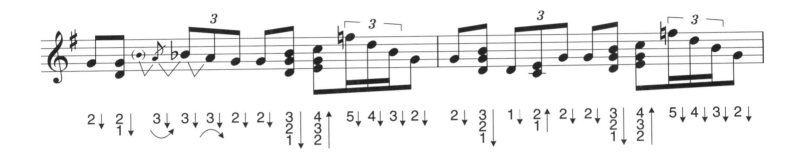

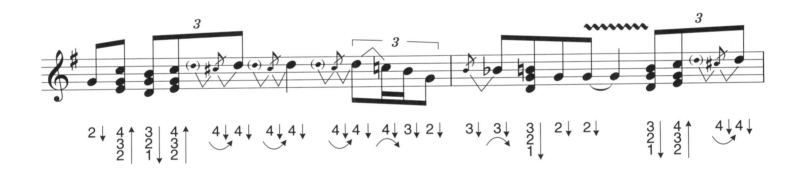

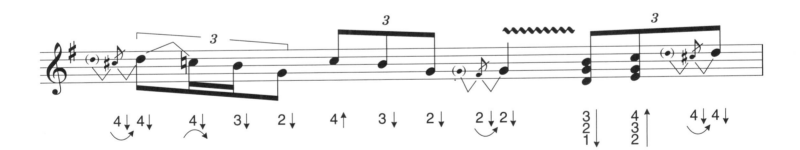

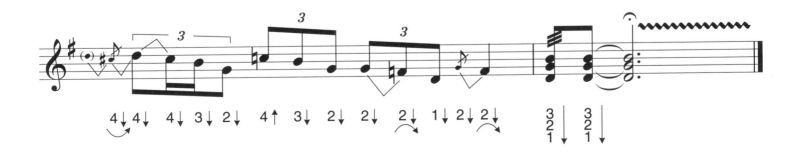

◆32 Outro Solo

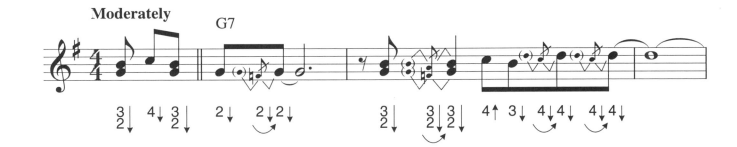

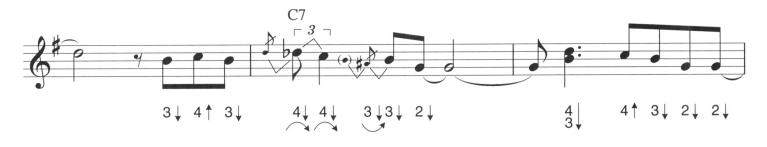

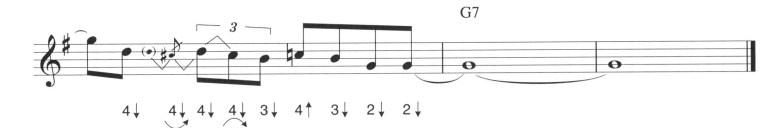

Notation Legend
For C Harmonica

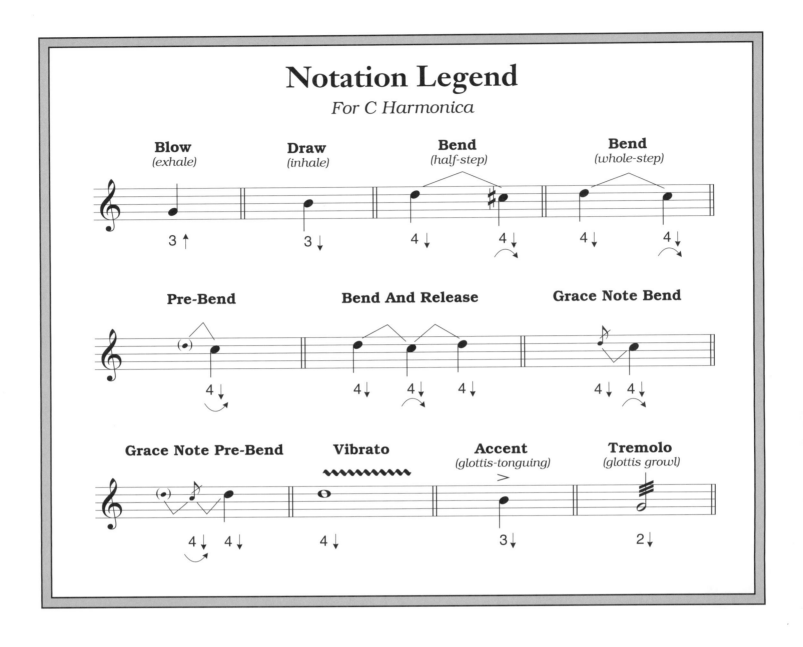

A Selected Discography

Albums

Even Dozen Jug Band	1964	Elektra EKS 7246
The Lovin' Spoonful *Do You Believe in Magic*	1965	Kama Sutra KLPS 8050
Soundtrack: *What's Up Tiger Lily?*	1965	Kama Sutra KLPS 8053
Hums of the Lovin' Spoonful	1966	Kama Sutra KLPS 8054
Soundtrack: *You're A Big Boy Now*	1967	Kama Sutra KLPS 8058
The Best of the Lovin' Spoonful	1967	Kama Sutra KLPS 8056
John Sebastian Songbook Vol. One	1970	Kama Sutra KSBS 2011
Woodstock: Music from the Original Soundtrack	1970	Cotillion SD3-500
John B. Sebastian	1970	Reprise RS 6379
Tarzana Kid	1974	Reprise MS 2187
Welcome Back	1976	Reprise MS 2249
The Best of John Sebastian	1989	Rhino R270170
Tar Beach	1993	Shanachie

As a Sideman (on harmonica)

Vince Martin & Fred Neil: *Tear Down The Walls*	1964	Elektra EKL 248
(Various artists): *The Blues Project*	1965	Elektra EKS 7264
Tom Rush: *Tom Rush*	1965	Elektra EKS 7288
Fred Neil: *Bleeker & McDougal*	1965	Elektra EKS 7293
Judy Collins: *Fifth Album*	1965	Elektra EKS 7300
Jesse Colin Young: *Youngblood*	1965	Mercury SR 61005
Tim Hardin: *Tim Hardin I*	1966	Verve 3004
Crosby, Stills, Nash & Young: *Deja Vu*	1970	Atlantic 7200
Gordon Lightfoot: *Sit Down Young Stranger*	1970	Reprise 6392
Everly Brothers: *Stories We Could Tell*	1972	RCA 4620
Woodstock Mountains: *More Music from Mud Acres*	1977	Rounder 3018
Laura Nyro: *Nested*	1978	CBS 35449
Happy Traum: *American Stranger*	1978	Kicking Mule 301
J. D. Souther: *You're Only Lonely*	1979	CBS 36093
Kenny Rankin: *Hiding in Myself*	1988	Cypress YL0114

Recently, John has also recorded with NRBQ, Graham Parker, Rory Block, Happy & Artie Traum and many others.

Suggested Listening for Blues Harmonica

Paul Butterfield

The Resurrection of Pigboy Crabshaw	1968	Elektra 74015
East-West	1968	Elektra 7315
In My Own Dream	1968	Elektra 74025
The Butterfield Blues Band/Live	1971	Elektra 2001 (2)

Jimmy Reed

Jimmy Reed At Carnegie Hall	1961	Vee-Jay 1035 (2)
Just Jimmy Reed	1962	Vee-Jay 1050

Sonny Terry & Brownie McGhee

Sonny And Brownie	1973	A & M 4379

Continue Your Studies With
John Sebastian!

This instructional CD and book was derived from John Sebastian's three-hour cassette course, **"Blues Harmonica"** produced by Homespun Tapes. If you enjoyed this CD, you will want to order the entire series to get more of John's remarkable insights into harmonica technique as well as detailed instruction for playing several of his popular tunes, including "Daydream," "Welcome Back," "Stagolee" and "Road House Blues." Three cassettes + TAB book: $29.95

John Sebastian Teaches On Video!
In addition to his audio cassette lessons, the best-selling video **"John Sebastian Teaches Blues Harmonica"** is available as well. On this lesson, John starts at the beginning, laying down a solid foundation for more advanced study. With special guest Jimmy Vivino (of the Conan O'Brien band). 80-minute video: $39.95

Also available for further study:

Harmonica Power! taught by Norton Buffalo
Video One – "Norton's Bag Of Tricks"
      90-minute video, $39.95
Video Two – "Blues Harp Techniques"
      80-minute video, $39.95

Note: Both videos can be purchased for the special package price of $69.95.

New Directions For Harmonica – Expanding Your Technique taught by Howard Levy
90-minute video, $39.95

These and hundreds of other top instructional tapes are available
from your music dealer, or directly from Homespun Tapes.
For complete catalog, write or call:

Box 694 • Woodstock, NY 12498 • (800) 33-TAPES

HOMESPUN
LISTEN & LEARN SERIES

THIS EXCITING NEW SERIES FEATURES LESSONS FROM
THE TOP PROS WITH IN-DEPTH CD INSTRUCTION AND
THOROUGH ACCOMPANYING BOOKLET.

NEW

NEW

GUITAR

Tony Rice Teaches
Bluegrass Guitar*

*A Master Picker Analyzes His
Pioneering Licks And Solos*

Tony Rice is known world-wide for his spectacular technique, brilliant improvisation and powerful soloing. In this lesson, he personally passes on to you the style he has developed during the two decades as the top bluegrass flatpicker of his generation. In careful detail, Tony analyzes licks, runs, solos and rhythm parts to hot bluegrass songs and fiddle tunes that will challenge and delight all flatpickers. Before long you'll be picking solos to the following essential bluegrass tunes: "The Red Haired Boy," "Little Sadie," "Your Love Is Like A Flower," "Blue Railroad Train," "Home From The Forest," "Wildwood Flower," "Old Train," "Wild Horse," and "Jersusalem's Ridge."

_____00695045 Book/CD Pack.....................$19.95

Happy Traum Teaches
Blues Guitar*

*A Hands-On Beginner's Course In
Acoustic Country Blues*

Take a lesson in fingerstyle blues guitar from one of the world's most respected teacher/performers. All you need to know is how to play a few basic chords to get started playing along with this user-friendly book/audio package. Beginning with the most basic strumming of a 12-bar blues pattern. Happy gradually starts adding fills, runs, turnarounds, bass rhythms and "boogie woogie" walking bass patterns that make the basic blues progression come alive. All of these elements are notated in both notes and tab.

_____00841082 Book/CD Pack.....................$19.95

Richard Thompson Teaches
Traditional Guitar Instrumentals*

*A Legendary Guitarist Teaches His Unique
Arrangements To Irish, Scottish and English Tunes*

Learn the techniques and style of traditional Irish, English and Scottish jigs, reels, hornpipes and other tunes arranged for fingerstyle guitar. On the CD, Richard explains how he uses altered tunings, string bends, vibrato as well as other techniques to give these tunes added "flavor." The book contains all of the songs and techniques written in notation and tab.

_____00841083 Book/CD Pack.....................$19.95

PIANO

David Cohen Teaches
Blues Piano

*A Hands-On Beginner's Course In
Traditional Blues*

Sit down at the piano and start to boogie. This easy play along course will have you rockin' and rollin' in no time – even if you have never played blues piano before. David Cohen (The Blues Project, Country Joe and the Fish, etc.) starts you at the beginning, quickly getting you into the elementary theory needed to understand chord progressions and the 12-bar blues form. Then it's right into setting up a solid left-hand rhythm in the bass to create a bedrock for the right hand improvisations to come. By the time this lesson ends, you'll be jamming the blues, plus you'll have a solid foundation on which to build.

_____00841084 Book/CD Pack.....................$19.95

HARMONICA

John Sebastian Teaches
Blues Harmonica

A Complete Guide For Beginners

A rock 'n' roll legend teaches you everything you need to play great blues harp in this unique lesson. John Sebastian starts at the beginning, carefully explaining the proper way to hold the instrument and make your first tones. John explains and demonstrates essential techniques such as reed bending, vibrato, rhythm grooves, "cross harp" playing and more as well as several great blues licks and complete solos. Lessons are written in notation and tablature.

_____00841074 Book/CD Pack.....................$19.95

PENNYWHISTLE

Cathal McConnell Teaches
Irish Pennywhistle

*A Hands-On Beginner's Course In Traditional Irish
Repertoire And Technique*

Learn to play traditional Irish songs on an instrument the whole family can enjoy. Cathal McConnell, known world-wide for his work with the popular Celtic band Boys of the Lough, teaches you the basics from the proper way to hold and blow the whistle, to the slurs, trills, rolls and other important techniques that will give you a truly Irish "feel." 12 traditional Irish folksongs are notated and explained in detail. As a bonus, the guitar accompaniment is recorded on one stereo channel while the pennywhistle is recorded on the other, so you can play along with only the accompaniment when you have mastered each tune.

_____00841081 Book/CD Pack.....................$19.95

FOR MORE INFORMATION, SEE YOUR LOCAL MUSIC DEALER,
OR WRITE TO:

HAL•LEONARD
CORPORATION

7777 W. BLUEMOUND RD. P.O. BOX 13819 MILWAUKEE, WI 53213

Contains tablature